The Bare Minimum Stretch Guide for Competitive S
Easy Stretches You can do at the Range to Up Your Game a.... .... r ain

By *Erin Garvin, M.S.*

Erin is an Exercise Physiologist with a B.S. and M.S. in Exercise Science and owns Empower Pilates and Yoga in Roanoke, Virginia. She is a master Pilates instructor trainer, yoga teacher, fitness instructor, Thai yoga therapist, and was voted a top ten Pilates Instructor for the worldwide *Pilates Anytime* contest. In addition, Erin has been featured in numerous national professional journals including *Women's Sports & Fitness, Pilates Style, Valley Business Front, Blue Ridge Outdoor Magazine, DirtRag,* and is a television fitness personality for a regional CBS affiliate. Her stretching for shooters articles have appeared in *FrontSight, The Tactical Journal,* and *Cowboy Chronicles.*

Erin competes in several shooting sports including the United States Pistol Shooting Association (USPSA), International Defense Pistol Association (IDPA), and Single Action Shooting Society (SASS). She is also a certified National Rifle Association (NRA) Pistol Instructor.

Erin has many fitness videos including *Gentle Stretching with Low Back Care; Foam Roller Muscle Release, Trigger Point Therapy, and Stretches on the Foam Roller; Strengthen & Lengthen: Full Body Pilates Mat Workout;* and *21-Day Fast Track to Sexy Sculpted Arms, Abs, and Back.* For more ways to stay flexible, strong, and reduce pain visit: *www.Empowerpilates.net.*

Dedication

This book is dedicated to Julie Kiser, friend, client, and fellow shooter who lost her life to breast cancer. This book is also dedicated to friend and fellow competitive shooter William "Babyface" Hancock who died much too young from heart disease. I would also like to honor Ron Avery, my first high-level shooting teacher, who passed away from cancer.

This book is outlined in the following manner:

Symbols in order of appearance:

= FITT Principles (Frequency, Intensity, Time, & Type)
= Breathing (Inhaling & Exhaling)
= Cues (How to perform a skill)
= Stretch (Identifies a different stretch)
= Muscles (Primary muscles stretched)
✓ **= Rationale (How it will help you)**
= Avoid (Don't do this)
= Postural Guidelines

Chapter 1. Welcome & Introduction

Congratulations on taking your first step toward improving your flexibility, easing the physical demands of shooting, and reducing pain and tightness. I wrote this book because competitive shooters repeatedly ask me for stretches to help them negotiate various shooting positions, minimize body tension, reduce pain associated with shooting, and improve posture.

Some fellow competitors nicknamed me "Slinky" as they watched me easily navigate and shoot from positions that they considered awkward. When your body is more relaxed and has less tension from forcing yourself into uncomfortable positions, you can more easily focus on executing shooting skills.

Higher level matches, in particular, often demand far-reaching leans, squatting to low ports and windows, assuming prone positions, reaching around barrels, and unusual body mechanics like hanging off a wall with one hand while shooting with the other hand. Having difficulty entering, exiting, and shooting from positions that demand a higher degree of flexibility translates to more time added to your score and possibly less accurate shooting, especially if muscles are shaking or trembling from being in difficult positions.

I am not suggesting that being more flexible is going to magically improve your shooting. Instead, obtaining a minimum level of flexibility will alleviate stress related to uncomfortable positions so you can better concentrate and execute your practiced shooting skills from an uninterrupted subconscious level.

From a muscle physiology perspective, having a base level of flexibility is critical for performance. With a proper stretching program, muscles achieve an optimal resting length which in turn maximizes their ability to contract. Muscles that are too tight or too loose cannot contract to their maximum potential. In addition, muscles that are chronically tight or inflamed inhibit opposing (antagonist) muscles to contract optimally.

Muscles that are overly tight can also create injury. For example, tight quadriceps are closely associated with hamstring tears. This means that a relatively simple task, such as sprinting from one shooting position to another, can possibly result in a muscle tear if one or more of the primary muscles or opposing antagonist muscles are too tight.

Finally, when muscle tightness continues to the point of chronic pain, atrophy (wasting away) may occur as a defense mechanism against further damage. Atrophy in turn can create muscular dysfunction which increases the chance of injury when attempting to perform demanding or explosive movements. Likewise, when a muscle is so tight that it doesn't fire appropriately, other secondary muscles will take on excess workloads to accomplish a physical task which can also result in injury.

Overly tight shooters with a muscular (mesomorph) build can greatly benefit from a bare minimum stretching routine to keep their muscles flexible enough to optimally contract, keep the opposing and secondary muscles firing, and stay out of pain so that atrophy, weakness, and dysfunction don't set in. On the contrary, shooters with a thin (ectomorphic) body type may have joints that tend to bend backwards (hyperflexible). Shooters with hyperflexible joints should focus on stability within the joints, using the muscles to stop the joint before hyperextension occurs so they can prevent further laxity to avoid loss of power and control or injury.

Most shooters looking to improve flexibility typically want a bare minimum of stretches that do not require a lot of time, hassle, or set up. The stretches outlined in this book have high benefit and low risk so that you can safely adopt whichever ones work for you.

Chapter 2: How to Stretch and Breathe

Before starting this program, let's review the FITT (Frequency, Intensity, Time, & Type) principles of exercise as they apply to stretching.

The FITT Principles for Stretching

🎓 **Frequency: 2-3 days per week**
🎓 **Intensity: To the edge of mild discomfort**
🎓 **Time: 20-30 seconds per stretch**
🎓 **Type: Static (after the muscles are warm)**

The FITT Principles Explained

🎓 **Principle Number 1 - Frequency: 2-3 days per week**

How often should you stretch? In reality, anything is better than nothing. Consider what your flexibility goals are and what realistic time you are willing to give to those goals. To improve flexibility, stretch two to three separate days per week. To reduce pain and tightness in problem areas, you may choose to stretch those specific areas more frequently, even daily or twice daily.

At first you may perform two or three different stretches each time you're at the range or after dryfire practice to build an associative habit. Try this frequency for 6-8 weeks and then reevaluate if the program is meeting your mobility needs. You can always add more stretches per session or stretch more frequently if you like.

In addition to stretching at the range or after dry fire practice, be creative in discovering what would normally be downtime during the day as an opportunity to stretch like while pumping gas, standing in line, travel breaks, or waiting for your coffee to brew. The main goal is to start stretching, then adjust based on how your program is meeting your goals.

🎓 **Principle Number 2 - Intensity: To the edge of mild discomfort**

Hold each stretch to the edge of mild discomfort so that you can gently encourage your muscles to lengthen without causing pain during the stretch. You should feel the stretch mostly in the belly of the muscle and not feel any intense sensations near the attachments or joints around the muscles. Listen to the feedback your body gives you. "If in doubt, leave it out" is a saying that means if you are unsure whether the intensity is too stressful, back off the range of motion or stop the stretch altogether. You want each stretch to feel like you could do a little more. This will keep you healthy, flexible, and free of injury.

You should be able to breathe easily in each stretch. If a stretch makes you hold your breath, back off the intensity a bit. Inhale and direct your attention to the muscles you are stretching.

Exhale and release any tension in the muscles you are stretching as well as any other areas of the body. Common areas that tend to tighten in response to stress are the upper trapezius (neck and top of shoulders), low back, and glutes. If you notice that you tighten these muscles inadvertently while stretching, it's likely you are contracting these muscles during other moments of perceived stress. The accumulated tension can lead to the gun shaking while shooting and chronic tightness in the body.

🎓 Principle Number 3 - Time: 20-30 seconds per stretch

Once you have chosen the stretches that work for you, hold each stretch for at least 20-30 seconds or up to 60 seconds for problematic areas. Some stretches can be bilateral (both sides) like a chest or shoulder stretch. Others can be unilateral (right/left) like a quadricep or triceps stretch. Performing several stretches for 20-30 seconds each doesn't take much time and is a great way to up your game and reduce pain. You can always add more stretches to your sessions to achieve more overall mobility. Stretching does not need to take long periods of time. As little as five minutes devoted to each stretching session can pay great dividends toward your shooting performance as well as overall health.

🎓 Principle Number 4 - Type: Static (after the muscles are warm)

There are all sorts of stretching methods like proprioceptive neuromuscular facilitation (contract/relax), active release stretching, and dynamic (moving) stretching. The most common type of stretching is static (fixed) stretching. Static stretching requires you to hold the stretch to the edge of mild discomfort for 20 to 30 seconds.

If your muscle relaxes holding a stretch, you can gently increase the range of motion. For ease and consistency, unilateral (single sided) stretches are explained using the right side. It is important to complete these stretches on the left side as well.

Muscles tend to respond better to static stretching after a gentle five-minute warm-up or following a shooting session that involves movement. Easy ways to warm the muscles include arm circles, push-ups, and brisk walking.

How to Breathe While Stretching

🫁 Breathing Guidelines

The most important consideration about breathing during each stretch is to make sure you do not hold your breath. Once you get familiar with not holding your breath, you can exhale to release tension in the muscle you're stretching and from other muscles that accidentally contract under stress.

In some stretches, the inhale facilitates spinal extension while the exhale facilitates activating the core which provides a protective bracing effect to the spine like an internal safety belt.

Linking breath with movement and focusing on the breath while stretching also restores balance in the parasympathetic nervous system (PNS), providing an environment for the body to heal. The following paragraphs will explain techniques along with cues for inhaling and exhaling.

Inhaling

While stretching, ideally you want to inhale through the nose to warm and filter the air. If you are congested or have difficulty breathing through the nose (e.g., deviated septum), then breathe through the mouth. Under stress, it's common to take short shallow breaths to the upper part of the chest or even hold the breath. To breathe more effectively, direct deep breaths toward the lower part of the torso which uses the diaphragm, the primary respiratory muscle. Diaphragmatic breathing calms the nervous system and brings stress hormones into balance. Diaphragmatic breathing can also be useful if you feel anxious or tense before a match. Breathing diaphragmatically helps get blood flow to the lower back which helps relieve pain and discomfort. This can be especially helpful if you are in a seated position for an extended period of time like a long drive to the range or match, sitting on a plane, or working at a desk.

Cues for Inhaling:
- To breathe diaphragmatically, place your hands on your belly and inhale inflating the belly so you feel it rise under your hand.
- The inhale is slow and smooth and shouldn't take too much effort or create stress in the body.
- Inhale diaphragmatically three to five times to get the hang of it.

Exhaling

At first, use the exhale to release tension from the body. As this gets more comfortable, try adding deep core activation to the exhale. Keeping your hand on the belly, exhale and pull the belly toward spine. Another way to learn core activation is to exhale as if you were blowing out a candle. This engages the transverse abdominals (TVA) that act as the inner safety belt of the spine protecting the back.

Often with pain or injury, the TVA muscles along with the supportive spinal muscles called the multifidi lose their ability to contract with appropriate timing when the spine needs bracing or protecting. Learning how to recruit the deep abdominals with this "pulling in" exercise helps retrain the abdominals and the multifidi when we need them for sudden positional changes and more challenging physical demands to decrease our risk of re-injury.

Cues for Exhaling:
- At first, exhale to release any unnecessary tension in the body.
- While relaxed, feel the abdominals tighten and pull inward during the exhale.

➡ Practice tightening the abdominals while exhaling without creating any unnecessary stress in the body.

➡ Try exhaling while pulling the abdominals in three to five times to get the hang of it.

Chapter 3: Shooting Stretches

This chapter identifies each stretch, lists the primary muscles stretched (see Muscle Anatomy diagram below), provides a rationale, lists important cues, and emphasizes movements to avoid for maximum benefit. Muscles tend to respond better to static stretching when they are warm. Stretch the muscles after a gentle five-minute warm-up such as arm circles, push-ups, brisk walking, or after a shooting session. As a reminder, use the FITT principles.

- 🎓 **Frequency:** 2-3 days per week
- 🎓 **Intensity:** To the edge of mild discomfort
- 🎓 **Time:** 20-30 seconds per stretch
- 🎓 **Type:** Static (after the muscles are warm)

Muscle Anatomy

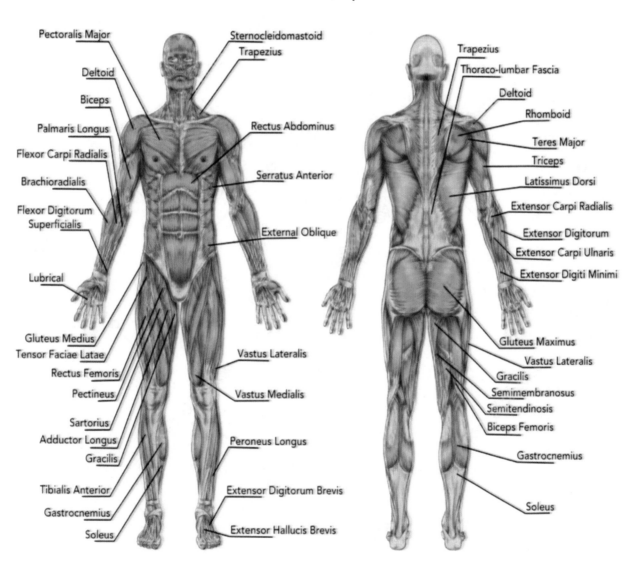

The Stretches

𝄐 _Stretch #1_: Standing Side Stretch

Muscles stretched:
🔧 Latissimus dorsi, intercostals, deltoid, obliques, quadratus lumborum, erector spinae, spinal multifidi, teres major

Rationale:
- ✓ Makes leans, reaching around barrels, fences, and barricades easier.
- ✓ Counteracts the forward position of shooting by opening the shoulders and back.
- ✓ Relieves lower back pain and tightness.
- ✓ Improves breathing by increasing intercostal flexibility between the ribs.

Cues:
- ▶ Lift both arms overhead and lengthen the spine up and to the right.
- ▶ Place the right hand on the right thigh to support your body weight.
- ▶ Inhale on the side being stretched allowing the muscles between the ribs to expand.
- ▶ Use the lower abdominals to pull the pubic bone up toward the navel and the front ribs downward to maintain the natural inward curve of the spine.

Avoid:
- ✋✋ Hyperextending the lower back.
- ✋✋ Elevating the shoulder blades.

🦅 _Stretch #2_: Standing Spinal Rotation

Muscles stretched:

🖐 Muscles along the thoracic, lumbar, cervical spine

Rationale:

✓ Makes reaching around barrels, walls, and barricades easier.
✓ Improves ease of shooting wide target transitions, especially in stand-and-deliver stages.
✓ Upper back rotation counteracts the forward stresses of shooting and prevents rounded upper back posture (kyphosis).
✓ Promotes healthy shoulders and neck.

Cues:

🖐 Stand with the right foot crossed over the left.
🖐 Inhale, lengthen the spine and lift the arms to a T position.
🖐 Exhale, rotate the spine to the right while looking toward your right hand.
🖐 Keep the shoulder blades down the back and the jawline parallel to the floor.
🖐 Pull the pubic bone up and front ribs down keeping the ribs over the pelvis.

Avoid:

🖐🖐 Hyperextending where the skull meets the neck.
🖐🖐 Hyperextending the lower back beyond its normal inward curve.

Stretch #3: Standing Spinal Flexion

Muscles stretched:

Erector spinae, rhomboids, quadratus lumborum

Rationale:
- ✓ Relieves postural muscle tension.
- ✓ Improves circulation in back muscles.
- ✓ Promotes torso mobility and stability.

Cues:
- Place feet shoulder-width apart.
- Bend the knees and place the hands on the thighs.
- Round the spine by pulling the pubic bone up, the front lower ribs down, and look toward the navel.
- Allow the arms to support the upper torso.

Avoid:
- Elevating the shoulder blades.
- Excess tension along the neck and shoulders.

Stretch #4: Standing Spinal Extension

Muscles stretched:
- Erector spinae, anterior deltoids, abdominals, pectoralis major, muscles along the thoracic, lumbar, cervical spine

Rationale:
- ✓ Relieves spinal muscles from the demands of shooting.
- ✓ Makes shooting from prone and low port positions easier.

Cues:
- Place feet shoulder-width apart.
- Bend the knees and place the hands on the thighs.
- Extend the upper back by lifting the sternum toward the sky.
- Gently lift the chin.

Avoid:
- Raising the shoulders toward the ears.
- Creating tension in the neck or tossing the head carelessly back.
- Hyperextending where the head meets the neck.
- Overly hyperextending the lower back.

Stretch #5: Triceps, Shoulder, & Lat Stretch

Muscles stretched:
- Triceps, deltoid, latissimus dorsi (top arm); Anterior deltoid (bottom arm)

Rationale:
- ✓ Relieves muscle tension in the arms, shoulders, and back.
- ✓ Reduces tension from the forward stresses of shooting.

Cues:
- Place a towel in your right hand.
- Raise the right arm, bend the elbow, and reach the right hand down the back.
- Reach the left hand up the lower back grabbing the towel in the right hand.
- Inch the hands closer together along the towel until you feel a stretch in the top arm (triceps and lats) and front of the shoulder (anterior deltoid) of the bottom arm.
- If your hands can touch without the towel, clasp the fingers together.
- Keep the shoulder blades down the back.
- Keep both shoulders open so neither roll forward.

Avoid:
- Slouching.
- Allowing the head to drift forward of the spine.

𝑓 ***Stretch #6:*** Rear Shoulder Stretch

Muscles stretched:

🦾 Posterior deltoid, rhomboids

Rationale:

✓ Relieves shoulder and upper back tension that occurs from holding the arms up while shooting.

✓ Makes shooting around walls, barrels, and hard leans easier.

Cues:

▬▶ Reach the right arm horizontally across the upper torso and use the left hand to hold the right upper arm in place.

▬▶ Keep the head over the spine so that the ears are in line with the shoulders from the side view.

Avoid:

🖐🖐 Slouching.

🖐🖐 Elevating the shoulders.

🖐🖐 Hyperextending the lower back beyond its normal curve.

Stretch #7: Front of Shoulders & Chest Stretch

Muscles stretched:
- Anterior deltoid, pectoralis major, biceps

Rationale:
- ✓ Counteracts the repetitive forward stresses that shooting places on the upper body and shoulders.
- ✓ Improves overall posture, shoulder, and neck health.
- ✓ Relieves upper back tension by decreasing how much the rhomboids have to work to counteract tight chest muscles.

Cues:
- Interlace your hands at the lower back or if they won't interlace, rest the hands as close as they will go toward each other.
- Lift the arms away from the back keeping the front of the chest and shoulders open.
- Keep the head over the spine so that the ears are in line with the shoulders from the side view.
- Jawline is parallel to the floor.
- Use the lower abdominals to pull the pubic bone up toward the navel and the front ribs downward to maintain the natural inward curve of the spine.

Avoid:
- Slouching.
- Raising the shoulder blades toward the ears.
- Allowing the head to poke forward of the spine.
- Hyperextending or creating tension in the back of the neck.
- Hyperextending the elbows beyond 180 degrees.

Stretch #8: Doorway Chest & Shoulder Stretch

Muscles stretched:
- Pectoralis major, pectoralis minor, anterior deltoid

Rationale:
- ✓ Counteracts the repetitive forward stresses that shooting places on the chest, upper back, and shoulders.
- ✓ Improves posture, shoulder, and neck health.
- ✓ Relieves upper back tension by decreasing how much the rhomboids have to work to counteract tight chest muscles.

Cues:
- ▶ Place the right hand shoulder height or slightly higher on a door frame or vertical structure.
- ▶ Walk forward leaving the hand behind until you feel the stretch across the front of the chest and shoulder.
- ▶ Keep the head over the spine so that the ears are in line with the shoulders from the side view.

Avoid:
- 🖐🖐 Poking the head forward.
- 🖐🖐 Allowing the front of the shoulder (humeral head) to push forward.
- 🖐🖐 Raising the shoulder toward the ear.
- 🖐🖐 Hyperextending the elbow beyond 180 degrees.

Stretch #9: Forearm Stretch with Elbows Bent

Muscles stretched:
💪 Anterior forearm

Rationale:
✓ Helps relieve the accumulated stresses shooting places on the wrists and forearms.
✓ May help prevent or relieve repetitive stress injuries.

Cues:
🔹 Place the palms together in front of the sternum in a prayer gesture.
🔹 Lower the hands until you feel a stretch on the inside of the forearms and hand even if the palms have to separate a little.
🔹 Keep the chest and front of the shoulders open.
🔹 Keep the head over the spine so that the ears are in line with the shoulders from the side view.

Avoid:
🖐🖐Allowing the shoulders to round forward.

Stretch #10: Underside of Forearm with Elbow Extended

Muscles stretched:
- Anterior forearm

Rationale:
- ✓ Helps counteract the accumulated stresses that shooting places on the forearm.
- ✓ May help prevent or relieve repetitive stress injuries.

Cues:
- ▶ Extend the right arm forward parallel to the floor with the palm facing the sky.
- ▶ Use the left hand to pull the right fingers down.

Avoid:
- Elevating the shoulders toward the ears.
- Hyperextending the elbow beyond 180 degrees.

Stretch #11: Top of the Forearm

Muscles stretched:
- ❥ Posterior forearm

Rationale:
- ✓ Helps counteract the accumulated stresses that shooting places on the posterior forearm.
- ✓ May help prevent or relieve repetitive stress injuries.

Cues:
- ➠ Extend the right arm forward parallel to the floor palm facing down.
- ➠ Use the left hand to pull the right fingers toward the underside of your forearm.

Avoid:
- ✋✋ Elevating the shoulders toward the ears.
- ✋✋ Hyperextending the elbow beyond 180 degrees.

𝄞 *Stretch #12:* Side Neck Stretch

Muscles stretched:
🖎 Trapezius, scalenes, sternocleidomastoid

Rationale:
- ✓ These muscles can be overly recruited while shooting or under stress.
- ✓ Excess tension in neck muscles can cause headaches, neck pain, and shoulder dysfunction.

Cues:
- ▶ Tilt the head sideways bringing your right ear toward the right shoulder.
- ▶ Use the right hand to gently assist the head closer toward the right shoulder while you reach the left hand toward the ground.
- ▶ Keep the shoulder blades down the back.
- ▶ Except for the neck, keep the rest of the spine vertical.

Avoid:
- 🖐🖐 Lifting the shoulders toward the ears.
- 🖐🖐 Leaning the body sideways.
- 🖐🖐 Aggressively stretching the neck.

Stretch #13: Diagonal Neck Stretch

Muscles stretched:
- Trapezius, levator scapula, scalenes

Rationale:
- ✓ These muscles can be overly recruited while shooting or under stress.
- ✓ Excess tension in neck muscles can cause headaches, neck pain, and shoulder dysfunction.

Cues:
- Stand tall, place your right hand on the back of the head just behind the left ear, and lower the chin diagonally toward the right side of the chest.
- Reach the left hand toward the ground.
- Except for the neck, keep the spine vertical.

Avoid:
- Aggressively stretching the neck.
- Leaning the torso.

✦ *Stretch #14:* Neck Rotation

Muscles stretched:
💪 Sternocleidomastoid, cervical spinal muscles

Rationale:
- ✓ Makes shooting around hard leans, barrels, and walls easier.
- ✓ These muscles can be overly recruited while shooting or under stress.
- ✓ Excess tension in neck muscles can cause headaches, neck pain, and shoulder dysfunction.

Cues:
- 👉 Stand tall, rotate the neck to the right keeping the jawline parallel to the ground.
- 👉 To increase the stretch, use two fingers on the jaw to encourage more rotation.
- 👉 Keep the chest and shoulders facing straight ahead.

Avoid:
- 🖐🖐 Rotating the torso.
- 🖐🖐 Aggressively rotating the neck.

Stretch #15: Back of the Neck Stretch

Muscles stretched:
- Trapezius, erector spinae, rhomboids, cervical spinal muscles

Rationale:
- ✓ Helps relieve tension that shooting and everyday life activities can place on the neck and upper back muscles.
- ✓ Excess tension in neck muscles can cause headaches, neck pain, and shoulder dysfunction.

Cues:
- Stand tall and tuck the chin (mouth closed) toward the chest until you feel the back of the neck and possibly the middle upper back stretching.
- Place hands on the back of the skull and gently pull the chin toward the chest.
- Bring the elbows toward each other under your face until you feel the stretch between the shoulder blades.
- Keep the ribs directly over the pelvis so the lower back has a natural inward curve.

Avoid:
- Lifting the shoulders toward the ears.
- Rounding the upper back.
- Aggressively stretching the neck.

∫ _Stretch #16:_ Quadriceps Stretch

Muscles stretched:
❧ Quadriceps including rectus femoris, vastus lateralis, vastus medialis, vastus intermedius along with psoas major, iliacus

Rationale:
✓ Helps reduce quadricep tightening associated with the explosive movements and running demands in shooting sports.
✓ Prolonged sitting can tighten the quadriceps and front of the hips.
✓ Eases knee and low back pain caused by tightness in the quadriceps and anterior hips.

Cues:
▪▶ While standing, gently pull your right foot toward the glutes.
▪▶ If you can't reach your foot, hold a towel in your hand and wrap it around the foot or ankle to hold the stretch.
▪▶ Keep the stretching thigh in line with the middle of the hip.
▪▶ Pull the pubic bone toward the navel and the front ribs down until the ribs are directly over the pelvis.
▪▶ Keep the hips level.

Avoid:
🖐🖐 Hyperextending the lower back.
🖐🖐 Letting the stretching thigh drift laterally.
🖐🖐 Allowing the foot or ankle of the stretching leg to turn sideways (inversion).
🖐🖐 Hyperextending the knee of the weight bearing leg beyond 180 degrees.
🖐🖐 Aggressively jerking the right foot toward the glute (may cause hamstring cramp).

Stretch #17: Hamstring Stretch

Muscles stretched:
- Hamstrings including biceps femoris, semitendinosis, semimembranosus

Rationale:
- ✓ Relieving tight hamstrings can decrease knee and lower back pain.
- ✓ Helps reduce hamstring tightening associated with the explosive movements and running demands in shooting sports.

Cues:
- Bend the left knee and sit back on the left side of the glutes.
- Extend the right leg forward and pull the right foot and toes toward the shin.
- Keeping the back long, hinge forward at the hips until you feel a gentle stretch throughout the back of the right thigh.
- Keep your weight shifted back as if someone were taking a chair further away from your glutes.

Avoid:
- Allowing the hip of the weight-bearing leg to deviate to the side (abduct).
- Creating too much tension under the knee or sit bone of the glutes.
- Hyperextending the knee of the stretching leg.
- Rounding the back.

🏃 *Stretch #18:* Inner Thigh Stretch

Muscles stretched:
💪 Adductor group including adductor magnus, gracilis, adductor longus

Rationale:
✓ Relieving inner thigh tightness can reduce knee and lower back pain.
✓ Adequate inner thigh flexibility allows for optimal stability and balance in dynamic positional changes required in shooting.

Cues:
▶ Bend the left knee and sit back on the left side of the glutes.
▶ Rest the hands on the left thigh while keeping the back long.
▶ Reach the right leg to the side and pull the right foot and toes toward the shin.
▶ Keeping the back long, hinge forward at the hips until you feel a gentle stretch in the right inner thigh.

Avoid:
🖐🖐 Hyperextending the knee of the stretching leg beyond 180 degrees.
🖐🖐 Creating too much tension behind the knee or sit bone of the glutes of the stretching leg.
🖐🖐 Rounding the back.

Stretch #19: Seated Hip Stretch

Muscles used: Deep external rotators including piriformis, obturator internus and externus, gamellus inferior and superior, quadratus femoris.

Rationale:
- ✓ Can relieve tension and pain in the hip and lower back.
- ✓ Prolonged sitting can chronically tighten the hip muscles.
- ✓ Helps reduce hip tightening associated with the explosive movements and running demands in shooting sports.

Cues:
- ▶ Sit in a chair or bench with the right ankle resting on or beyond the left thigh.
- ▶ Keeping the back long, hinge the torso forward until you feel a gentle stretch.
- ▶ Pull the pinky toe toward the shin to protect the knee.

Avoid:
- ✋✋ Rounding the back.
- ✋✋ Allowing the top ankle or foot to turn sideways (inversion).

♪ *Stretch #20:* Calf Stretch

Muscles stretched:
- Gastrocnemius

Rationale:
- ✓ Relieves tightness on the back of the lower leg, ankle, and foot.
- ✓ Assists with balance, stability, and abrupt starting and stopping demands for explosive position entry and exit.

Cues:
- ▶ Standing tall, place the foot with the toes pointed up against an upright object like a post or wall.
- ▶ To increase the stretch, press the hips toward the wall.

Avoid:
- 🖐🖐 Hinging at the hips.
- 🖐🖐 Allowing your glutes to get farther away from the wall.
- 🖐🖐 Hyperextending or bending either knee beyond 180 degrees.
- 🖐🖐 Aggressively stretching the calf.

Stretch #21: Shin Stretch

Muscles stretched:
🦵 Tibialis anterior, anterior ankle and foot

Rationale:
✓ Relieves tightness on the shin, top of the ankle, and foot.
✓ Assists with balance, stability, and abrupt starting and stopping demands for explosive position entry and exit.

Cues:
▶ While standing, cross the right leg in front of the left leg placing the top of the right toes on the floor (toenails on the ground) next to the outside of the left foot.
▶ Bend the left knee until you feel the front of the right shin stretching.
▶ Ease into the stretch to prevent foot cramping

Avoid:
✋✋Turning the stretching ankle or foot sideways (inversion).

𝒦 *Stretch #22:* Squat

Muscles stretched:
🔱 Quadriceps, hamstrings, glutes, hips, adductors, lower back, gastrocnemius, soleus

Rationale:
- ✓ Eases the challenges of low ports, kneeling, and low shooting positions.
- ✓ Can help relieve low back pain and tightness.
- ✓ Can reduce lower body stiffness.

Cues:
- ▥▶ Place the feet shoulder-width apart with the toes pointed slightly outward.
- ▥▶ Keeping your weight on the heels, bend the knees and hips to lower your glutes as close to the ground as possible.

Avoid:
- ♛♛ Allowing the knees to drift inward.
- ♛♛ Permitting the inner arch of the feet to collapse toward the ground.
- ♛♛ Shifting your weight forward on the toes.

Chapter 4: Guidelines for Good Posture

While some postural skeletal structure is genetically determined, much of it is influenced by personal habits, mimicking others, repetitive activities, and by overall affect or mood (i.e. mood begets posture and posture begets mood.)

Poor posture places undo wear and tear on the bones and intervertebral discs and creates excess tension on compensatory muscles. To combat these issues, the following guidelines provide suggestions to alleviate pain, improve mobility, and reduce stress.

Postural Guidelines:

- Body weight is evenly distributed on the four corners of the foot: mound under the big toe, pinky mound, inner heel, and outer heel. Many people weight the big toe or pinky side of the foot too heavily.

- Feet are pointed straight ahead or slightly outward.

- Inner arch of the foot is lifted (not collapsed).

- The Achilles tendon on the back of the lower leg is vertical.

- Knees are relatively straight and not hyperextended beyond 180 degrees.

- Hips are level and not shifted to one side (like someone holding a baby on a hip).

- Ribs are directly vertical over the pelvis and not flaring in the front or slouched behind the pelvis.

- If you tend to overly extend the lower back (extreme lordosis), use your abdominals to pull the pubic bone upwards toward the navel to place the lower spine in a more natural slightly inward curve.

- The upper arm bones are gently externally rotated with the thumbs facing front, creating a wide-open chest.

- Shoulder blades gently rest down the back without elevating the shoulders near the ears.

- The upper spine is lifted as if a helium balloon were attached to the head pulling you toward the sky without thrusting the ribs forward.

- From a side view, the ear is in line with the shoulder and the jawline is parallel to the floor.

🧍 From a side view, the mid shoulder is in line with the middle ribcage, side hip bone (greater trochanter), knee, and outside ankle bone (lateral malleolus).

By practicing good posture and staying mobile, you can diminish body tension, reduce pain, and make shooting from awkward positions easier.

With Appreciation,
Erin Garvin

Bibliography

Eizenberg, N., Briggs, C., Adams, C., & Ahern, G. (2008). *General anatomy: Principles and applications*. Sydney, Australia: McGraw Hill Education.

Alter, M. (2004). *Science of flexibility (3rd Ed.)*. Champaign, IL: Human Kinetics.

Australia American Council of Exercise. (1991). *Personal training manual*. Sydney, Australia: Human Kinetics.

American Council of Exercise. (2011). *ACE group fitness instructor manual: A guide for fitness professionals* (3rd Ed.). San Diego, CA: American Council of Exercise.

Anderson, B. (2010). *Stretching: 30th Anniversary Edition*. Bolinas, CA: Shelter Publications.

Coulter, H.D. (2002). *Anatomy of hatha yoga: A manual for students, teachers, and practitioners*. Honesdale, PA: Body and Breath Inc.

Kendall, H.O. (1971). *Muscles, testing and function (2nd Ed.)*. Baltimore, MD: Williams and Wilkins.

Grimaldi, A., Richardson, C., Durbridge, G., Donnally W., Darnell, R., & Hides J. (2009). The association between degenerative hip joint pathology and size of the gluteus maximus and tensor fascia lata muscles. *Manual Therapy, 14*(6), 611-617.

Kim, H. (2019, September 1). *Practical Shooting Training Group. Managing Recoil Series* (Video File). Retrieved from https://www.practicalshootingtraininggroup.com/training-videos/

Kraftsow, G. (1999). *Yoga for wellness: Healing with the timeless teachings of viniyoga*. London, UK: Penguin Compass Books.

Lett, A. & Diaz, K. (2016). *Stretching on the Pilates reformer: Essential cues and Images*. Montreal, Quebec: Rebus Press.

McAtee, R. & Charland, J. (2007). *Facilitated stretching*. Champaign, IL: Human Kinetics.

Riebe, D., Ehrman, J., Liguori, G.,& Magal, M. (2018). *ACSM's guidelines for exercise testing and prescription (10th Ed.)*. Philadelphia, PA: Lippincott Williams & Wilkins.

Thank You

Thank you to the following people for their help with this project: Michael Maina for editing and stretching photographs, Ben Stoeger, Kimberly Eakin, and Greg Zachman for their review and feedback, Liv Kiser at Livtophoto for the cover photographs, and Lisa Lusk for her creative input.

Made in the USA
Lexington, KY
16 December 2019